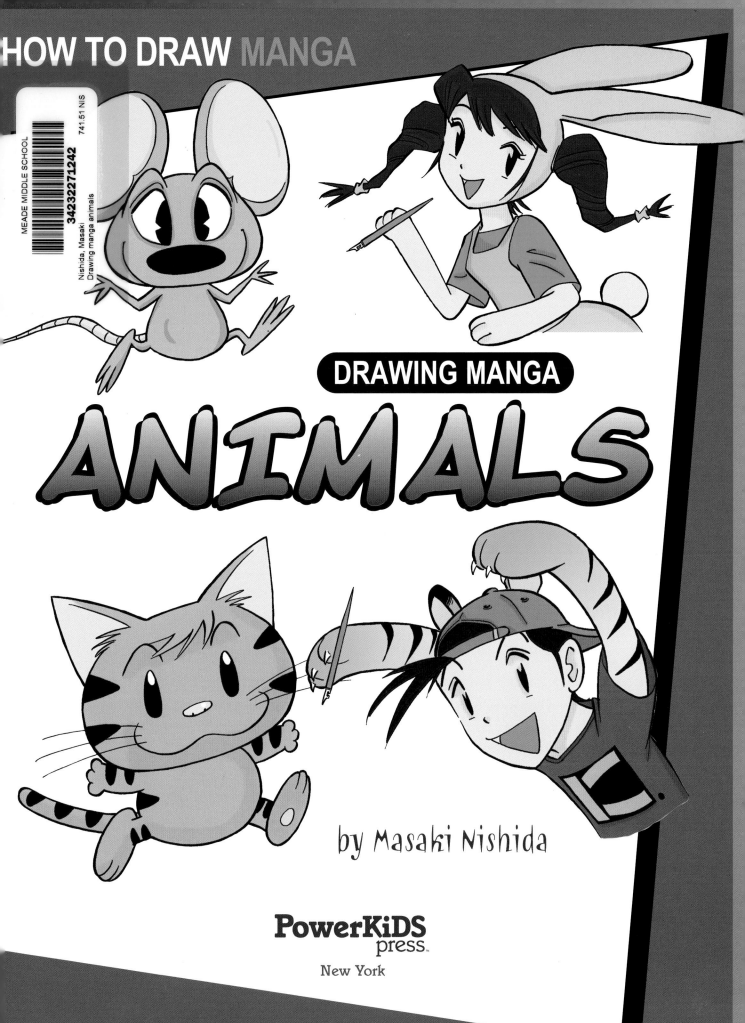

## DRAWING MANGA
# ANIMALS

by Masaki Nishida

**PowerKiDS** press.

New York

Published in 2008 by The Rosen Publishing Group, Inc.
29 East 21st Street, New York, NY 10010

First Edition

American Editor: Dean Galiano
Japanese Editorial: Ray Productions
Book Design: Erica Clendening
Coloring: Erica Clendening, Julio Gil, Thomas Somers

Manga: Masaki Nishida

Photo Credits: p. 23 (Cat, Dog, Mouse, Horse, Rabbit) © Photodisc; p. 23 (Marlin) © www.istockphoto.com/Andrew Hyslop; p. 23 (Tiger, Lion) © Digital Stock.

Library of Congress Cataloging-in-Publication Data

Nishida, Masaki, 1960-
  Drawing manga animals / Masaki Nishida.   \ 1st ed.
     p. cm.   \ (How to draw manga)
  Includes index.
  ISBN-13: 978-1-4042-3846-6 (library binding)
  ISBN-10: 1-4042-3846-8 (library binding)
 1. Animals in art  \Juvenile literature. 2.  Comic books, strips,
etc. \Japan \Technique \Juvenile literature. 3.
Cartooning \Technique \Juvenile literature. 4. Drawing \Technique \Juvenile
literature.  I. Title.
  NC1764.8.A54N57 2008
  741.51 \dc22
                              2006037232

Manufactured in the United States of America

# CONTENTS

# About this Book

**H**i! I am Masaki. That's my friend Sayomi on the right. In this book we are going to show you how to draw manga animals step-by-step.

**I** am a manga artist. I draw all kinds of manga stories, such as sports, history, and adventure. I have always loved reading and drawing manga.

**M**anga is a **unique** Japanese art form. Its style looks a little like an American **comic book**. Manga often borrows story ideas from American and European movies. Manga has always been popular in Japan. Today manga is enjoyed by people all over the world.

**M**anga style combines pictures and **text** in an exciting way. This is manga's biggest **attraction** because it makes it easy to follow the **plots** of the stories. You will learn to draw eight manga animals in this book. You will also learn how to use these characters to tell a manga story. Are you ready to enter the manga world?

You will need these supplies to draw manga animals:
- A **sketch** pad or a sheet of paper
- A pencil
- A pencil sharpener
- A ballpoint or a fine felt pen
- An eraser

In this book, Masaki and Sayomi will show you how to draw manga animals. They will also show you how to **illustrate** a manga story.

Once you learn the basics, you can recreate the manga animals and stories in this book. Your new drawing skills might even give you the inspiration to make up stories and characters of your own.

Hi! My name is Sayomi. Manga animals are fun to draw! Masaki and I will show you how.

# DRAWING A CAT

"Cats make great pets!"

"Let's draw a happy cat!"

First draw an oval shape for the head.

**1**

**2**

Now draw two triangles for the ears.

**3**

Add a smaller circle for the body. Now draw rectangles for the arms, legs, and tail. Add circles for the hands and ovals for the feet.

**4**

Now it's time to draw in the face and details such as hair and toes.

**5**

Ink only the lines you want to keep. Erase all pencil lines once the ink is added.

**6**

The cat is almost done! Finish the final details and color your cat however you like!

# CAT AND MOUSE

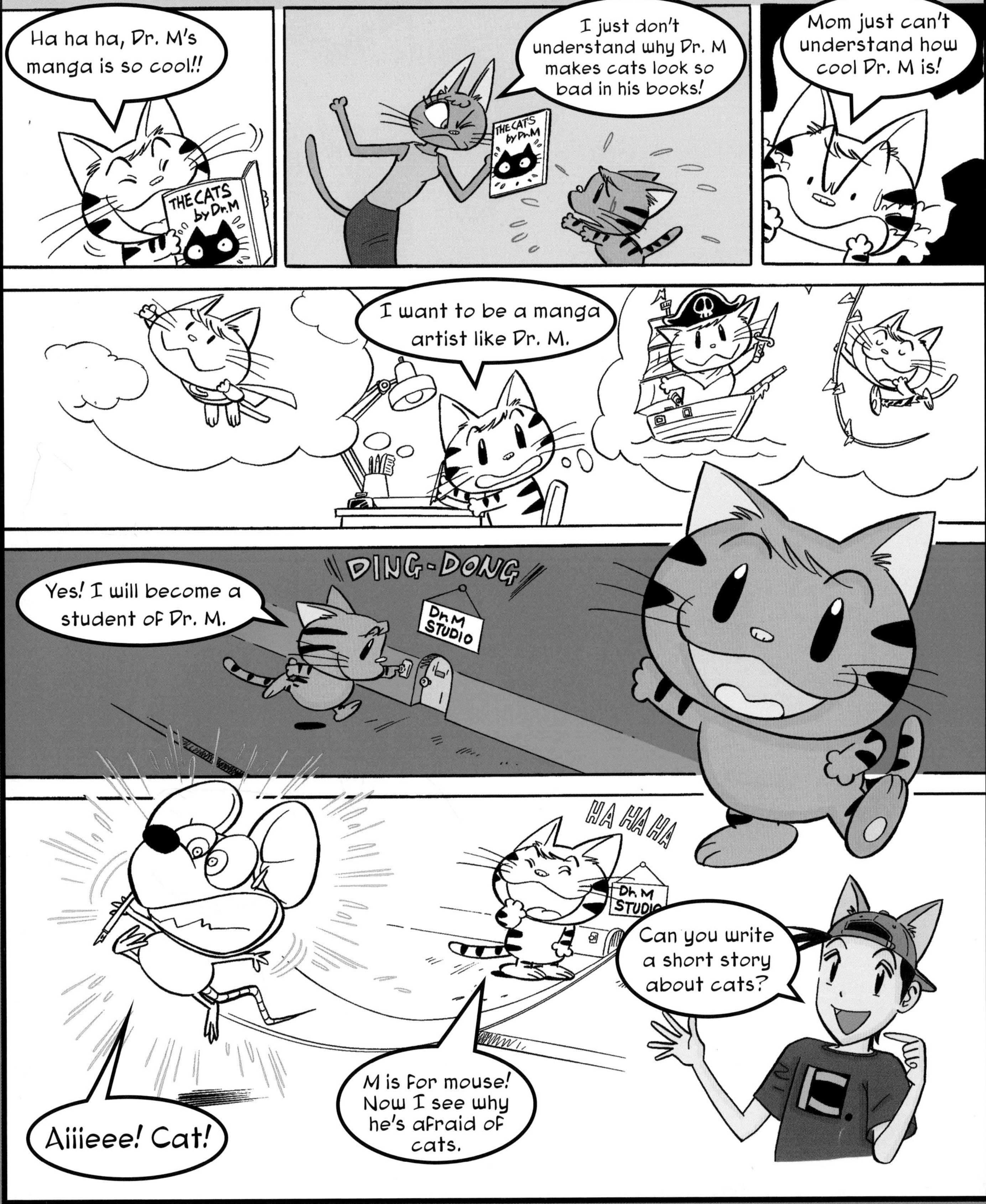

# DRAWING A
# MOUSE

I think they are cute!

Who says mice are pests?

Start with the head.
An oval works best.

1

2

Add two more ovals
for the big ears.

3

Draw an oval for
the body and
rectangles
for the arms and legs.
Don't forget to add the hands, feet, and tail!

4

5

It's time to add the
face and the fingers
and toes. Draw the
detail in the ears.

Ink the lines you
want to keep. Erase
any extra lines.

6

Once the shading
and the color is
added, we are done!

# DRAWING A HORSE

Time to round up a story about a horse.

Howdy, partner!

Draw a rectangle for the head.

**1**

**2**

Add two more rectangles for the neck and body.

**3** Add the legs using rectangles and circles. The ears and the hooves are triangles. Draw the tail as well.

**4** It's time to add the horse's face and mane.

**5** Ink the final lines and erase the pencil lines.

**6** Almost done! Just add the shading to the hooves and the color.

# DRAWING A MARLIN

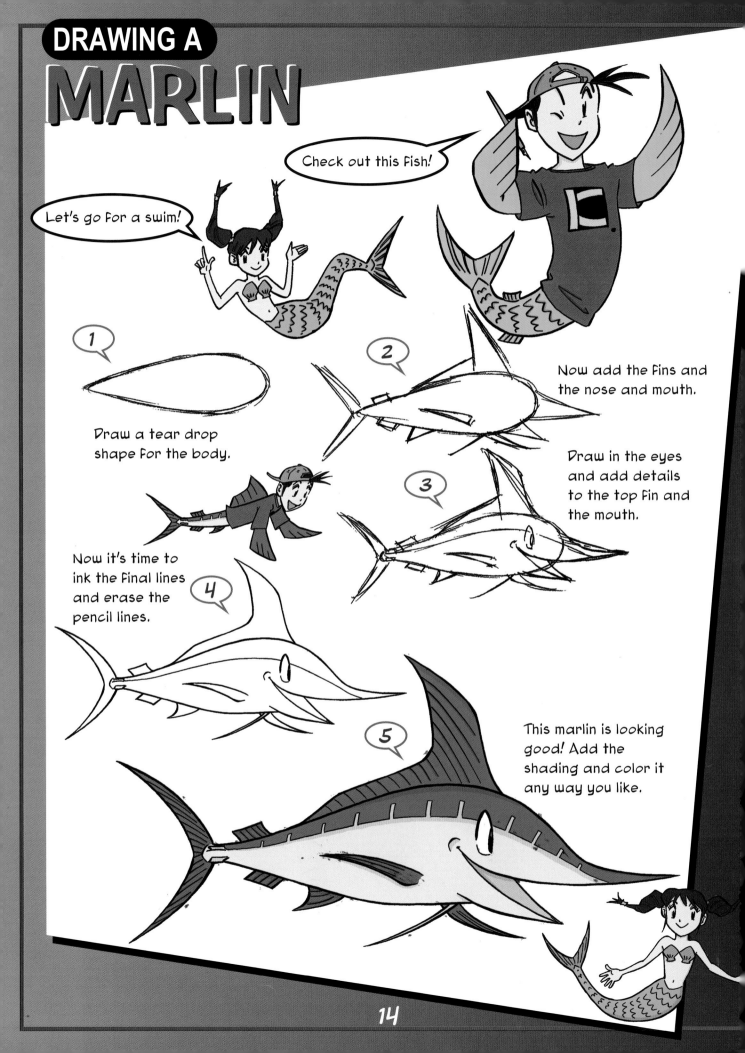

**Check out this Fish!**

**Let's go for a swim!**

**1** Draw a tear drop shape for the body.

**2** Now add the Fins and the nose and mouth.

**3** Draw in the eyes and add details to the top Fin and the mouth.

Now it's time to ink the Final lines and erase the pencil lines.

**4**

**5** This marlin is looking good! Add the shading and color it any way you like.

# MARLIN TO THE RESCUE

# A RABBIT'S RIBBON

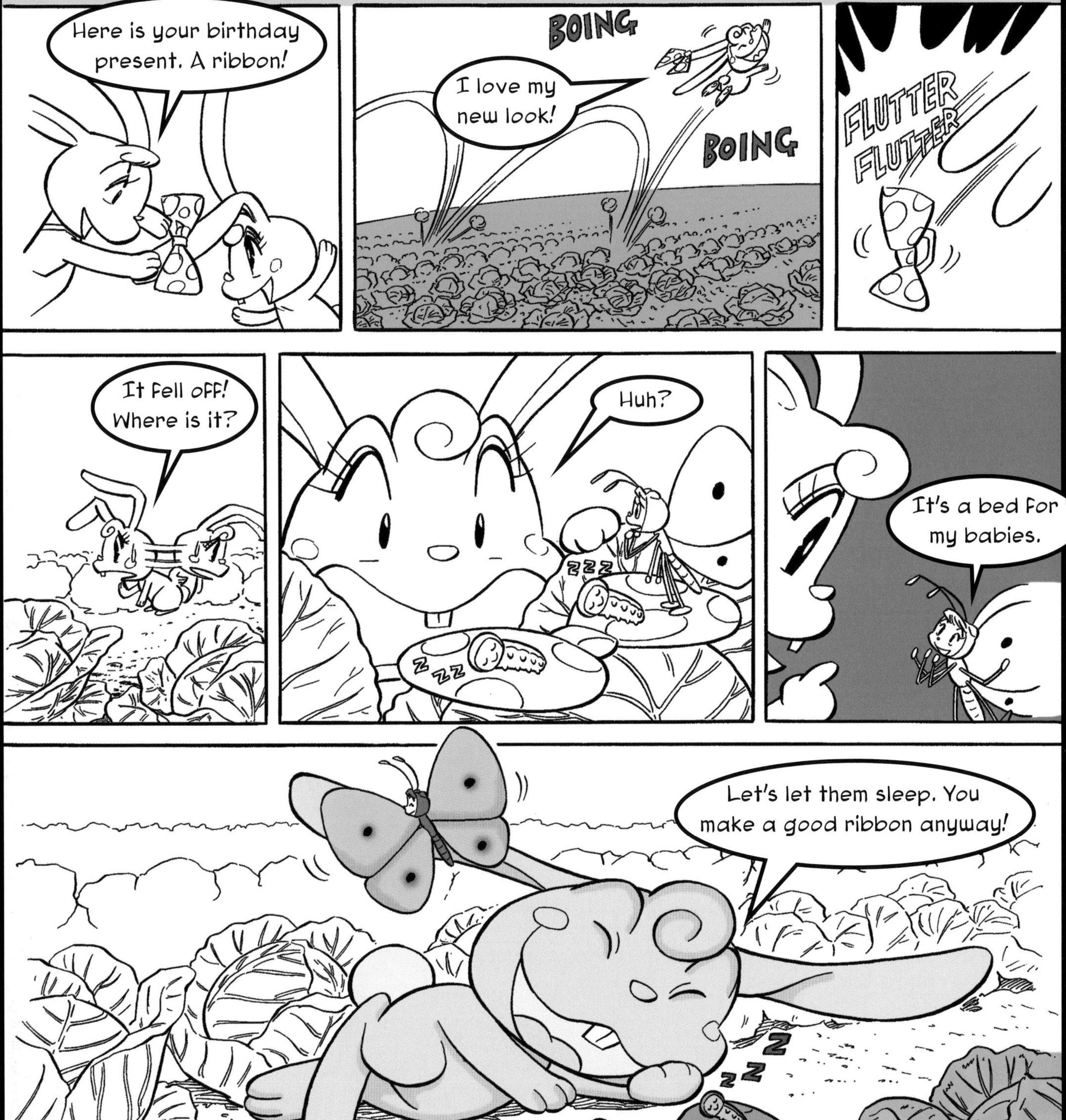

# DRAWING A TIGER

**Roooaarrrr!**

**1** Start with the head. An oval works best.

**2** Add small circles for the ears and a rectangle for the body.

**3** It's time to add the hands, legs, and feet. Don't forget the tail.

**4**

**5** Draw in the face and add details. Ink your final lines.

**6** Color the tiger any way you like.

18

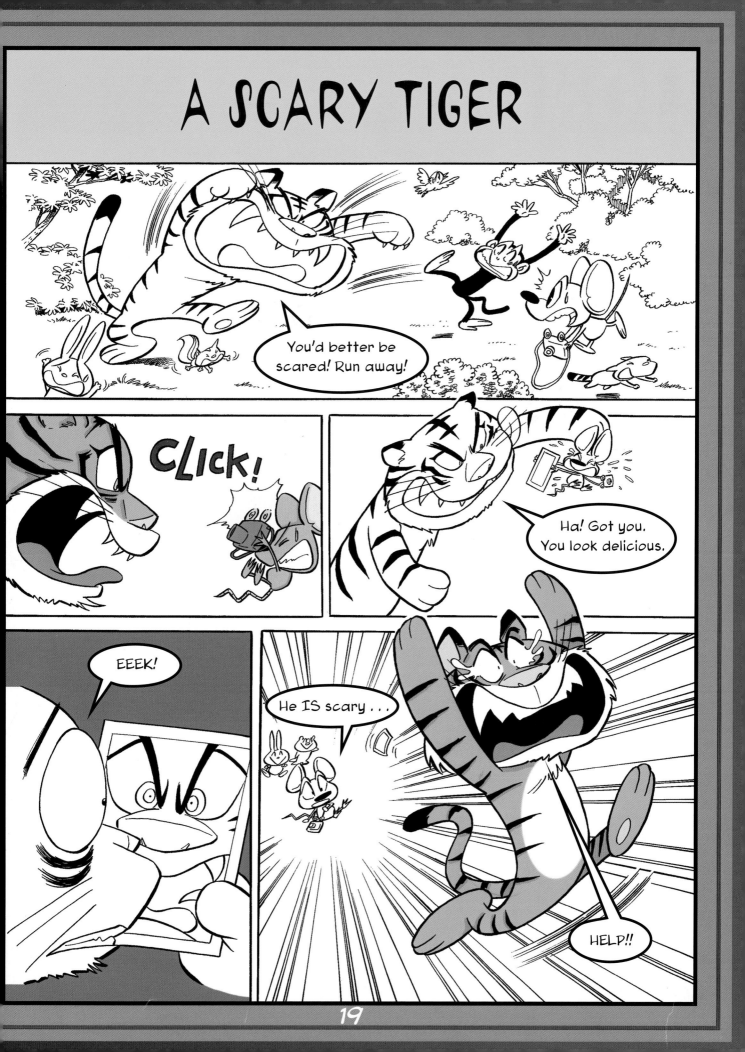

# DRAWING A LION

**I am the king of the beasts.**

**No, I'm the king!**

**1** Start by drawing an oval for the head.

**2** Add two smaller ovals and the body.

**3** Now add the arms, legs, hands, and feet. Draw the tail and ears as well.

**4** It's time to add the face and more detailed lines.

**5** It looks good! Now ink your final lines and erase the pencil lines.

**6** Color the lion and you're done!

# GLOSSARY

**attraction** (uh-TRAK-shun) Pulling something together or toward something else.

**carnivorous** (kahr-NIV-er-uhs) Describing an animal that eats other animals.

**comic books** (KAH-mik BUHKS) Books with drawings that tell a story.

**exceed** (ik-SEED) To go beyond the limits of.

**herbivorous** (hur-BIV-er-uhs) Describing an animal that eats plants.

**illustrate** (IH-lus-trayt) To create pictures that help explain a story, poem, or book.

**inspiration** (in-spuh-RAY-shun) Powerful, moving guidance.

**omnivorous** (om-NIV-er-uhs) Describing an animal that eats both plants and animals.

**plots** (PLOTS) The events that happen in a story.

**sketch** (SKECH) A quick drawing.

**species** (SPEE-sheez) A single kind of living thing. All people are one species.

**text** (TEKST) The words in a piece of writing.

**unique** (yoo-NEEK) One of a kind.

# Meet the Animals

### Cat
Species: *Felis catus*
Life Span: Up to 15 years
Weight: Up to 11 lbs (5 kg)
Diet: Mainly carnivorous

### Marlin
Species: *Makaira nigricans*
Life Span: Up to 15 years
Weight: Can exceed 2,000 lbs (907 kg)
Diet: Carnivorous

### Dog
Species: *Canis lupus*
Life Span: About 12 years
Weight: Up to 154 lbs (70 kg)
Diet: Mainly carnivorous

### Rabbit
Species: *Oryctolagus cuniculus*
Life Span: About 5 years
Weight: 2-4 lbs (1-2 kg)
Diet: Mainly herbivorous

### Mouse
Species: *Mus musculus*
Life Span: Up to 6 years
Weight: .4-1.5 oz (12-30 g)
Diet: Omnivorous

### Tiger
Species: *Panthera tigris*
Life Span: About 22 years
Weight: Up to 700 lbs (317 kg)
Diet: Carnivorous

### Horse
Species: *Equus caballus*
Life Span: About 25 years
Weight: Up to 2,000 lbs (907 kg)
Diet: Herbivorous

### Lion
Species: *Panthera leo*
Life Span: About 15 years
Weight: Up to 500 lbs (227 kg)
Diet: Carnivorous

# INDEX